IF YOU WANT AN ENEMY, TRY TO HELP SOMEONE

IF YOU WANT AN ENEMY, TRY TO HELP SOMEONE

JOHN CHANCEY KINGSTON

Copyright © 2023 John Chancey Kingston.

All rights reserved. No part of this book may be reproduced, stored, or transmitted by any means—whether auditory, graphic, mechanical, or electronic—without written permission of both publisher and author, except in the case of brief excerpts used in critical articles and reviews. Unauthorized reproduction of any part of this work is illegal and is punishable by law.

Library of Congress Control Number: 2013915670

ISBN: 979-8-89031-604-2 (sc)
ISBN: 979-8-89031-605-9 (hc)
ISBN: 979-8-89031-606-6 (e)

Because of the dynamic nature of the Internet, any web addresses or links contained in this book may have changed since publication and may no longer be valid. The views expressed in this work are solely those of the author and do not necessarily reflect the views of the publisher, and the publisher hereby disclaims any responsibility for them.

One Galleria Blvd., Suite 1900, Metairie, LA 70001
(504) 702-6708
1-888-421-2397

CONTENTS

Acknowledgment ix
Introduction xi

Chapter One	My Cousin Lennie.	1
Chapter Two	She Is Not Family	4
Chapter Three	Helping the Homeless	8
Chapter Four	You Are Making Us Look Bad.	12
Chapter Five	Did You Take It?	16
Chapter Six	The Highest Penalty for Helping.	18
Chapter Seven	Knife Wounds from Desert Sand.	20
Chapter Eight	Church Members.	24
Chapter Nine	The High Cost of Independence	27
Chapter Ten	That Old Car.	32
Chapter Eleven	A Chilly Game Changer	36
Chapter Twelve	More Agonizing than Any Enemy	39
Chapter Thirteen	I Dropped My Cell Phone	41
Chapter Fourteen	Distinguishing Between a Helper and an Enemy	48
Chapter Fifteen	The Enemy from Beyond.	56
Chapter Sixteen	When A Man Does Not Want.	59

Conclusion 63
Ten Points of Enemies and Help 65
Instructions for the Glass Test. 67

In Memory of the Ultimate Helper,
ALLEN WAYNE THOMPSON,
my very missed longtime good friend,

Perhaps the best C-5 Galaxy Aircraft
Mechanic assigned to the
United States Air Force Reserve
433 Military Airlift Wing

Favorite Quote of Allen:
*"If You Hang Around 9 Broke Ass Guys,
You Will Be the 10th One"*

Gone Too Soon
February 17, 1963 - August 9, 2016

ACKNOWLEDGMENT

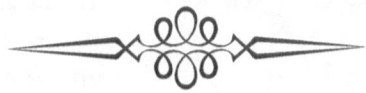

The inspiration for the title and content of this book was birthed from a conversation I had with my brother-in-law and friend Anthony Dewayne Kiser. From time to time, Anthony and I engage in conversation, sharing stories of life events. On one occasion, while conversing with Anthony about an encounter I experienced with an acquaintance, I called my friend *Sonny*. Sonny was someone I helped but, as you will witness, caused the help to stop once he allowed his own unfounded distrust to invade the situation. This book's title dawned on me after I explained to Anthony what had transpired with Sonny and the echo of his only response: "Chance, I'm going to tell you what an old woman told me many years ago. Her words were 'If you want an enemy, try and help someone.' At that time years ago, it did not make sense to me, and I did not agree with her position because I felt it was too negative. However, I would agree with her today." Within minutes of concluding the conversation with Anthony, I started this book.

I have to thank my longtime friend Allen W. Thompson for his selfless efforts in facilitating a communication with his childhood friend and published author Tony Hardy.

I must also thank my wife, Gwendolyn, for her very professional suggestions and revises. Her tireless crafty edits and skillful proposals made this manuscript stir in a positive fashion in which it would not have if she was not involved.

I have to also thank the very artistic designer of this book's cover my daughter Erica. Her skills and imagination of the skull design and colors of a deceptive recipient of help has captured the essence of this books continent and title.

The names of each chapter reflect the experience of the moment in time. I have expounded upon chapter 7 with an additional life-experiences book soon to come. It is a trilogy that bears the same name as the chapter entitled Knife Wounds from Desert Sand: Dark Wars behind Contractor Support in Iraq.

INTRODUCTION

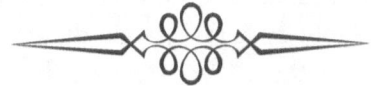

My wife and I have been happily married for more than forty years. We have a daughter, a son, six granddaughters and two grandsons. We are in our early sixties and in very good health. I still have my father who is very much in the land of the living and four healthy siblings. So, I am sure it is very easy to see why I consider myself extremely blessed. But that is only the tip of how I have been positioned in life. I make this proclamation because of the broad nature of the many skills, crafts, and life experiences I possess. I am usually in a good position to help someone, and often, I do. You see, the more I help, the more I am blessed.

Help can come in a variety of methods. It may come in the form of a whisper of advice while at other times by presenting an opportunity, a small monetary contribution, or simply providing a glass of water. But the most self-fulfilling assistance for me to render someone occurs when I provide help that will last far longer than a simple gift of money, because money simply runs out. An example of this is an old but powerful expression that implies, "If you give a man a fish, after he eats it, he will come back for another one as soon as his hunger returns. But if you teach a man to fish, he will be able to feed himself for a lifetime."

From time to time, we all attempt to help one another. But sometimes, the recipient of the help will find a way to blame the helper if the situation turns out unexpectedly bad, even if the helper has no control of the outcome or, even worse, the recipient has asked for assistance. Most times, the recipient will conjure up thoughts like "You must be up to something if you freely help" or "Nobody helps anyone these day unless there's something in it for them." Why can't it be as simple as you (the helper) are only following the golden rule of treating your neighbor as you would want to be treated? Often the results are either you make an enemy, make them angry, or at a minimum, make them uneasy. In some instances, there are some people you simply just cannot help.

Throughout the years, the stereotypical image of help is a young man (often a Boy Scout) helping an old lady cross the street. But what if while he is helping her, a car recklessly speeds through the intersection and hits her? Did he help her, or was he part of the problem? Should it be said that he actually caused her to be in that location when danger struck?

In another example, a man meets a stranger who is in need of a skill the man possesses. The man decides to help the stranger solely because he is passionate about the skill and decides to teach the stranger the skill for free. But because the help was without charge, the receiver did not embrace the assistance, and thus, the help was gone forever.

There is a wise old proverb that expresses, "keep your friends close, but keep your enemies closer. "I have always heard that the passage means keep your enemies close because they may harm you, but your friends may need to be kept closer because often the ones you call friends are not your friends at all, but merely someone who cannot wait to betray you. Therefore, friends may require closer scrutiny.

At the conclusion of this book, you should be able to keep the many dangers of simply assisting someone to a minimum or at least identify and avoid many hurdles encountered while attempting the noble task of helping someone by understanding when, how, why, and who you should help and who you should not.

After the conclusion, it is recommended that you participate in taking the glass test. Please be advised that before taking part in the test, it is recommended that all participates join in only if all steps are followed, because the results can be frightening.

Chapter One
MY COUSIN LENNIE

After serving six years in the military, I decided to separate from the military and move back home to position myself and assist in the family business. I had to adapt to a different financial regime because at this time, the steady stream of military income was not present. It was during this time that my cousin Lennie, who lives in Jackson, Mississippi, frantically called me on the phone early one morning, exclaiming that he desperately needed to borrow $300 or *they* were going to get him and he would be going to jail. Lennie assured me he would repay the loan the next time he comes to town (which happened to be the upcoming weekend for Mardi Gras). I asked Lennie who were the *they* that he spoke of, but he never clarified his comment with a straight answer. I bounced the possibility of approving the loan to Lennie by my bank president (my wife), and she approved it.

Lennie did not come to town that weekend or any weekend for months. In fact, Lennie did not return until our family's annual Thanksgiving dinner nine months later. Immediately when Lennie saw me, he extended greetings to me then reminded me that he had not forgotten about the money I had loaned him. Though he was extremely overdue with the return of the money, I resolved that since he at least acknowledged the debt, he had every intention of repaying the loan the *next time* he was in town.

When that *next time* occurred, he greeted me with the same original comment as before: "I haven't forgotten about the money you loaned me." This greeting continued for several years, at the same event, Thanksgiving dinner. Finally, after about six years in another setting but being met with the same greeting, I calmly responded, "Lennie, you need to just stop." Surprisingly, Lennie responded in a loud, aggressive voice, "So what do you want to do?" I questioned, "What are you talking about?" Lennie motioned toward me. "What do you want to do?" he repeated in a louder, threading tone. I held my stance and composure then calmly questioned, "If I am getting you right, you want to fight me over the money that you owe me?" He repeated again, "I just want to know what you want to do." At this juncture, I was floored. Then I voiced, "Wow, you can't be serious. If it means that much to you, maybe you just need to keep it. We don't have to fall out about that money."

All jokes aside, Lennie took me to school that day. If anytime a person showed that they were now an enemy after you helped them, this was the test-case model. This was the first time I had loaned money to a family member who was not a sibling. There is a lot to be said concerning the old saying, "You can choose your friends, but you can't choose your family." This particular cousin literally wanted to fight me over the money that he owed me. I would have saved myself a lot of grief if I had known that when it comes to family members, or even friends, only loan what you can afford to give.

But there was a surprise twist that would soon come. About six months later, Lennie paid the entire loan in full; it was six years late, but he paid it. I am not sure what caused him to settle up, but I suppose he replayed the events that occurred in his mind, and his conscience would not release him. I have loaned money to other family members, and at least half have never repaid, but never did I have any of them so quickly turn into an enemy as my cousin Lennie.

Chapter Two
SHE IS NOT FAMILY

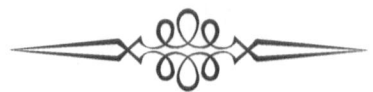

During the early 1990s, after making it home from a routine workday, my wife approached me with a humble look on her face as she began to fill me in on a conversation she had with one of her brothers earlier that day. She revealed that John had called her from his home in Lake Charles with a favor to ask. I quickly responded with a question, "OK, how much money does he want to borrow?" She quickly steered me in a different direction by letting me know it was not that type of favor. My wife further explained that John was asking the favor for his wife's sister, Lorraine. She had been offered a job in the town in which we lived. Lorraine wanted to accept the job but did not have the necessary funds needed to secure an apartment right away. Therefore, John wanted to know if we would accommodate Lorraine at our home until she earned enough to get an apartment. After hearing the narrative, I questioned my wife as to the length of time we would be consenting to for this favor. My wife's reply was "about five weeks." I had one last question for my wife, "Have you ever met Lorraine?" "No, but if John is asking on her behalf, she must be OK," she responded. Without hesitation, I replied, "I suppose you are right. If we did not help in this situation, it would feel sort of wrong because she is just a person in need of help. In fact, she is almost family." We both agreed to allow Lorraine temporary residence in our home for the time specified while she started her new job.

Prior to Lorraine's arrival, we informed the children of our plans and asked for their input. The children assured us that they did not mind the new arrangements. Lorraine arrived about three days later. It was good to have a visitor from our hometown and, at the same time, render help as well. We made provisions for Lorraine in our daughter's room. In exchange, my daughter, eight, and my son, six, had previously agreed to share the bunk beds that were in our son's room. We went over a few house rules and shared expectations; we never mentioned anything about charging her to stay with us. Our only concern was to help someone who was trying to move forward with their life.

It didn't take long for things to take a sour turn. The same day Lorraine received her first check, I came home to find our refrigerator stocked full of beer. We had not given Lorraine any house rules to follow about alcohol; I just thought she would have been mature enough to ask if it was OK to bring alcohol into what she knew was an alcohol-free home. We were not drinkers, and that was only common courtesy. Prior to that day, Lorraine never bought any extra food. When meals were prepared, she was always invited to eat with us or choose any other item from our kitchen. Thus, my thoughts were, if anything was to be placed in our fridge, it should have been cleared first. However, after I informed her of my issue with the beer in our home, the beer was removed. That problem was solved, right?

A few days after the beer incident, another dilemma would find its way into our household. My wife informed me that Lorraine came frantically running into the house, crying and babbling about her car being repossessed. She explained that Lorraine was visited at her job by someone trying to repossess her car, but she had managed to avoid repossession by leaving work. By the time she reached our house, my wife described Lorraine as hysterical while begging her to hide the car in our backyard and pleading for us to loan her $200 to pay the bank for the car. The one day I needed to be reached at my job, my wife couldn't. She tried to reach me to consult with me about the situation and the loan, but she was unable to contact me that day. Therefore, after several attempts to reach me and my wife witnessing Lorraine's behavior and predicament, she reluctantly made the decision to loan the money. I hit the roof when I found out. But I could only hope that by loaning her the money for her transportation, she would continue to get to work to make the money she needed to eventually pay us back and achieve her original goal of getting an apartment.

About a week or two later, my wife discovered cigarettes in an ashtray in my daughter's room. Oddly enough, we had to explain to a thirty-year-old why it was not a good idea to smoke in our eight-year-old daughter's room in a smoke-free house. My wife and I got through to her that night, or at least that was what we thought. But about three days later, there was an even stronger smell of smoke in my daughter's room. By now it was time to give her what she has earned—exit instructions. I told her that she had six days to find a place to live; in two days, she left a forwarding address and was gone. The exit was peaceful, and I presume it was because deep down, she knew she had overstepped her bounds. But maybe it was simply because there were items already ordered being shipped to our address. Nevertheless, that was a good day because the person that started out as almost family turned into just an invader.

Liberation! We thought that would be the last we would see of her. Unfortunately not—about ten days later, a long-distance phone bill arrived that revealed numerous calls Lorraine had made while lodging with us. Needless to say, she never got permission to make those calls and did not pay that bill or the loan.

However, what she did do with great zeal was tell her family what horrible people we were and how impossible it was to live with us because we were monsters that were too controlling. She also accused us of looking down on people. We made her feel small, and we took delight in it. None of the problems she caused or any of the irresponsible actions she participated in was ever part of the commentary that made it back to us. No surprise, this is usually the nontruth version of the story that most delusional people use. We were now in the enemy category with Lorraine. What was an otherwise cordial relationship with Lorraine's mother prior to her stay with us and our relationship with John's wife (Lorraine's sister), her lies to her sister and mother put us in the enemy category with them as well. How's that for helping someone? How's that for creating an enemy? We opened up our home to Lorraine and treated her just like family, but she proved to us that she clearly was not.

Chapter Three
HELPING THE HOMELESS

When I see a homeless person or a panhandler down on their luck, I have been known to buy meals or at least pass on a few dollars his or her way. Some would say that there are too many scam artists out there just waiting on someone like me who will freely hand over a dollar; well, that is not my concern. I am more concerned that I may pass a person who really does need a few dollars or a meal. So be it if someone happened to get a meal or a few dollars out of me through trickery, then that person just got me. That minor charity will not change much with me, but for some, this could be their breaking point. I guess I inherited a charitable character from my parents, and from all indications, this same character was passed on to my children.

My niece and nephew have become very crafty investors in real estate. The beauty of their business is that they began their operation with the principal service to others. From its inception, many of their friends, as well as strangers, have gained from the business, whether it was a job or home to help out a friend or a homeless person going through tough times. For several of the recipients, without the help, they would not have had a home.

Another aspect of the business success is my niece's and nephew's abilities to form alliances that mutually benefit all participants. Case in point is the occasion when my nephew met a family that spoke very little English. Their sole income source was driving their old pick-up truck around the city, gathering then later selling old scrap metal. During this encounter, my nephew informed the family that he had a lot of old debris on one of his properties in need of moving. He offered the family the opportunity to move the debris, and in doing so, all the metal was theirs to keep. This was a huge windfall for this family, so they eagerly accepted the offer and accomplished the task that same day. That chance meeting started a strong alliance that would quickly benefit both sides. That family became the newest members on the payroll, removing debris from houses. In turn, the family not only got paid for their work, they had a constant supply of all the scrap metal they could get their hands on free of charge.

Several weeks into this newly forged alliance, my nephew discovered that the family's home was not much more than a hut. The overall structure of the dwelling was deplorable. The roof leaked, the walls were perforated with multiple holes, making it impossible to control the temperature, and the floor was about as close to a dirt floor as you can possibly imagine. From the appearance of things, the $150 a month they were paying for this very substandard housing was too much.

After seeing the condition of this family's living quarters, my nephew devised a plan that would be mutually beneficial for all. He and my niece had a vacant house in a very good neighborhood that needed rubbish removed from it. It also needed some minor carpentry work. Outside of the fact that the house needed minor repairs, it was still far better than the house this family currently lived in. As well, this house would easily rent for about $1,000 each month. Therefore, they both agreed and offered the family rental of the house at the same rate of their current rental of $150 and some additional stipulations:

- They would be responsible for clearing out the dwelling.
- They would be making the minor carpenter repairs.
- They would continue the before-agreed-upon task of removing rubbish from houses obtained by the business as well as cashing in on any scrap metal free of charge.

From its inception, the nomadic family did not hold up their end of the agreement. They never paid rent, and they never made any repairs. However, they were always available to remove debris because there was always scrap metal available to them. Once I became aware of this outrageous abuse of kindness, I informed my nephew that in spite of this family's money problems, he needed to engender the family to honor the agreement; otherwise, he was asking for problems.

Six months later, there still were no paid rents or repairs made. Apparently, by this time, the family felt vested into their new home because when the stove malfunctioned, the tenants had no problem requesting my nephew to fix it. Hence, in the name of helping, and since my nephew could not bear to evict them, he asked me to inspect the stove and make any needed repairs. With the initiative of assisting those in need, I honored the request and repaired the stove.

A few more months passed and still no rent had been collected and no repairs had been made. It was in the heat of the summer when the air-conditioning system went out, and of course, the tenants demanded it be repaired. Finally, my nephew decided to draw the line. He concluded that there was no way he was going to spend money on a family that would not pay rent. Consequently, he informed them that once the rent was paid, he would repair the air-conditioning unit.

Finally, the family would experience a little discomfort and make some changes, right? Wrong. They were used to no air-conditioning, and since they were in a much better house than they had before and paid no rent, they decided to ride it out as long as they could. Also, to add insult to injury, they displayed anger and agitation with the fact that my nephew would require them to finally honor their agreement. It appeared that they thought they were entitled to keep the house rent-free indefinitely. So my words of earlier finally came full circle, and my nephew finally had to evict them. Before the family exited the property, they stole everything they could get their hands on (attached or not) from the house and created thousands of dollars in damage to the home. Housing assistance will not stop an enemy from being crafty even when there exists an honest attempt to help.

Chapter Four

YOU ARE MAKING US LOOK BAD

Aunt Sadie lived in a small city about seventy miles away from my wife and I. Aunt Sadie is the much younger wife of my late great-uncle Lester. This story took place years after my great-uncle Lester had been lost at sea as a merchant marine, leaving Aunt Sadie to continue to raise their six children on her own. These children are adults now, all in their late thirties and early forties. Her youngest (Sherman) and her middle (Hendry) sons still live with her. Often, whenever my wife and I were in Aunt Sadie's town, we would usually stop in for a visit.

Hendry, Aunt Sadie's middle son, had been a drug abuser for years. Before the drug abuse, Hendry was out of the house on his own, doing his own thing, but the drug abuse brought him back home. Between the highs and lows of his drug use, Hendry would often kick in the doors and break out the windows of the home. In addition, Hendry would riddle off disrespectful language to his mother and steal and pawn Aunt Sadie's personal possessions. This behavior would often produce fights between the two sons because the youngest, Sherman, would not just stand by and watch Hendry destroy all his mother's property or, worse, verbally abuse her.

Sometimes I witnessed Hendry's reckless behavior while visiting with Aunt Sadie. On one of our visits with Aunt Sadie, she warned me of the abuse of Hendry telling the police that he was me when he had no identification. Other times, I was made aware by Aunt Sadie herself every time I made my routine phone calls to her to see how she was doing. During one of our phone calls, Aunt Sadie revealed to me that she had to call the police on Hendry because he got into a fight with Sherman. She went on to say that she had not seen him since that night. I inquired further by asking my aunt why Hendry and Sherman were fighting. Aunt Sadie replied, "Because Hendry said that he was the man of this house and told Sherman that he'd better get in line. Then he called me a battle-ax and told Sherman . . . 'that old battle-axes don't run things here, I do.'" She went on to say that after hearing endless ranting from Hendry, Sherman had reached his boiling point, and as a result, Sherman pounced on Hendry. "I had no choice but to call the police before they killed each other, but by the time the police arrived, Hendry had run off." I responded, "Aunt Sadie, run off or gone is where Hendry needs to be. His action screams to you that he is no longer your son. He is a guy who looks like the guy you identify as your son. He is a person that is only a shell of who Hendry once was. So until he gets some help with his addiction, he needs to be permanently banned from your house." The pain of absorbing my words and realizing the truth about her son was too much for her to bear. She began to sob then uttered, "But he has nowhere to go."

I felt compassion for my aunt that day, but I also felt compelled to emphasize the point that if she did not have Hendry removed from her house, things would only get worse, and at some point, she would be forced to make a stand against Hendry. Weeks later, I was astonished to discover that the solution that Aunt Sadie came up with would have never been a viable option. Aunt Sadie owned a free and clear house that was purchased years ago by her husband as he started to build for his retirement. The house was being used as rental property. The property served as her only source of income outside of a meager pension provided for her by her late husband, Uncle Lester. Aunt Sadie did the only thing she felt she could do; she decided not to renew the lease to her current tenants and moved them out. She then welcomed her new tenant, her drug-infested son. I guess it is a matter of perspective how one would conclude this move, which could be categorized as love for a child, utter desperation, or just foolishness.

My wife and I continued to visit my aunt over the next few years. She was always glad that we took the time to come and see her. On one of our visits, Aunt Sadie asked if she could borrow $350 for some much-needed dental work. It was income tax season, and she promised the money would be returned in three weeks upon receipt of her income tax refund check. My wife and I both knew that if we relied on any of her six children to pitch in to take care of the funding to repair their mom's teeth, she probably would have never received the needed funds. Call me stupid if you like, but to be perfectly honest, I thought that she was going to return the money once she received her income tax refund. I thought wrong. If only some of the Court TV shows were aired back then, I would have known how this would have turned out—the same as it does on the show. Whenever people tell you that they will pay you when they receive their income tax check, what they are really telling you is that you will *never* get your loan returned.

It was a loan, and yes, I would have liked it returned, but this situation was much bigger than $350. She needed money for her teeth, and I would have easily just given her the money, especially since she probably had little other options. Still, as time passed, we continued our visits with Aunt Sadie, but the loan never came up. My aunt never mentioned it, and neither did we.

Months later, at a family gathering, I was excited to see two of Aunt Sadie's children. I had not seen them for quite some time, so I greeted them with a cheerful salutation. To my surprise, my cheerful greeting was met with rudeness and sarcasm. These were my cousins; I was puzzled as to why I was greeted in such a cold and distant manner. I mentioned my encounter with my cousins to one of my siblings. My brother told me that prior to my arrival to the function, Aunt Sadie had received numerous compliments from the family on how well her teeth looked. He continued by describing how Aunt Sadie genuinely praised me and my wife for paying for her dental work. As he chuckled, my brother remarked, "When her children found out that you and Gloria had loaned their mother money for dental work, three of them made it clear they had a problem with it, because of the negative comments they made about how you and your wife think you are all that. But I would not give much credence to their ramblings because they are hating on you because they know you stepped up and handled business by blessing their mother, and it should have been done by them."

Chapter Five
DID YOU TAKE IT?

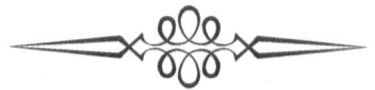

A tornado destroyed the house in Oklahoma that my aunt left to my uncle Elroy. Uncle Elroy lived several states away and therefore relied totally on his brother Fred's assessment as to the level of the damage. Uncle Fred's conclusion deemed the destruction was quite severe, and he suggested to my uncle Elroy that he demolish the entire structure and build a new one. Elroy was not easily convinced of Fred's conclusion; thus, two weeks later, Elroy arrived in Oklahoma to view the damage for himself. After which, he agreed that starting over was the only option.

Once the insurance claim was finalized, Uncle Elroy was equipped with enough capital to rebuild a new home at the same location. Knowing Fred's background in carpentry, Elroy solicited Fred to assist him in the project to rebuild. Fred was self-employed and had many contractor connections (brick masons, plumbers, roofers), which kept the cost of the construction to a minimum. Two weeks into the project, Elroy had to return to his job, leaving Fred with the task of foreman.

While Elroy was in town, he paid $50 a day to some building laborers. Once Elroy left town, Fred paid everyone out of his bank account since Fred did not leave any operating funds. After two weeks of paying the laborers and buying supplies, Fred contacted his brother and presented him a bill of $2,000. Reluctantly, Elroy paid the bill, but his contention all along was that he couldn't understand why the bill was so excessive. Elroy was being unrealistic. He did not take into account the position he left Fred in to manage the entire project, including funds and wiring of the entire house. In addition, Fred had to drastically reduce his own business hours and operation to make the project happen.

The project was completed after four months of diligent work. Six months later, while Uncle Fred was engaging in a casual conversation with my great-uncle, my great-uncle asked, "Did you take money from Elroy's house project?" Though stunned by the question, Fred explained to my great-uncle how Uncle Elroy left town, leaving him as project manager without funds. Fred further explained how Elroy had an issue with him when he requested reimbursement of his personal funds. Once my great-uncle heard Fred's side of the story, he expressed disgust about the way Elroy was trashing Fred and that he needs to get a clue about what things cost and the value of help.

Unfortunately, this was not the last time Fred would have to explain or hear of ill-spoken words from various family members concerning Fred's extended helping hand. However, this incident did not stop Fred's willingness to help family members. But in Fred's own words, "you have to pick the family you decide to help, because in many cases, they don't know how to receive it, and when they don't, instead of thanking you for the help, they make you the enemy by slaying you with their tongue."

Chapter Six

THE HIGHEST PENALTY FOR HELPING

I worked as a contractor in both Iraq and Kuwait to support the war effort. While in Iraq, I was confined to the base for obvious reasons—there was an enemy lurking outside of it. But life was totally different in Kuwait because Kuwait was not a war zone.

In Kuwait, I lived off base in the civilian community. It was an inimitable experience for many reasons: for one, I learned many of their customs. At the end of a long, hot summer workday, I had just exited my vehicle in the apartment parking lot when a taxi pulled up in front of my apartment. Suddenly, the back door of the taxi opened, and an Arab man who was seemingly semiconscious rolled out of the taxi and lay lifeless on the ground. No one rushed to help him. My natural instincts urged me to help, but in observance of those gathered around, I somehow knew that I shouldn't. I felt there was a good chance that this was one of their rituals. No one even blocked the sun from beaming on him for about five minutes. The cab driver and other passersby just watched. Gradually, the man began to come around. Once the man started to show strong signs of life, someone provided shade and water. Slowly the crowd began to dissipate.

The following day at work, I mentioned the episode to one of my coworkers who had been in the Middle East far longer than me. He explained that in Kuwait and other Middle Eastern countries, everything is done *Inshallah*, meaning "Allah willing" (God willing [hopefully]). The belief dictates that everything is in God's hands, and if anyone were to interfere with a person when Allah may or may not be about to take them, the interferer could be held responsible.

If a person is ever held accountable for someone's death due to interference, the family of the deceased person can sometimes receive wages from the one who interfered equal to what their loved one would have earned if he would have lived a full life. So it is easy to see that a lifetime of blood money can be quite expensive. In many cases, until blood money is paid in full, a person is not allowed to leave the country. The person may not become your enemy, but the long-haul cost of helping under these conditions can be far more severe and, perhaps, the highest penalty for helping.

Chapter Seven

KNIFE WOUNDS FROM DESERT SAND

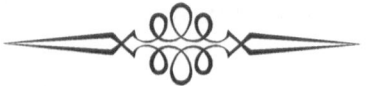

In the previous chapter, I mentioned one of the religious practices carried out in the Middle East that probably seems a bit strange to most of you. But there were other strange practices that occurred by American contractors I associated with as we supported the war effort overseas. Contracting work in the Middle East proved to be more unique than any of my other work experiences. But the cultural difference of the region is not the focus of this chapter; its focus is the attitude and temperament of my American team members.

I was selected to lead a team of five after the former leader could no longer withstand the outside temperatures of the region. Our job was to remove electronic jamming systems from military convoy vehicles once the vehicles exited the Iraqi war zone. At the time of this appointment, I was fifty years old and a prior team member. The average age of my team members was about forty-three. However, with the nature in which most of them carried out their occupational duties, it appeared I was in charge of leading children. From all my past civilian and military experiences, I knew that when a leader is promoted over his or her peers, there is often a problem. Soon after I settled into the new position, I was told I had changed. Truly, the only thing that changed was I was now responsible for the work getting done.

On a normal day, we usually worked between ten and twelve hours, seven days a week. One day, during my first week after being appointed leader, there were about thirty trucks waiting for jammers to be removed. The work was going well, that is, until Axel stated, "We were happier when Lester was in charge." At that moment, the work stalled as the crew waited with anticipation to see how I would respond. I responded calmly, "What would you like me do with that?" Axel continued, "I am just saying we were happier when Lester was in charge." I then responded, "Do your job, collect your pay, and then you can be happy." Axel was relentless. He continued to be disruptive, so much so that he left me no alternative than to contact higher management. It took this measure to finally curb his irrepressible attitude. Work on the convoy vehicles resumed, and we were finished by noon. Since the workload was low that day and no additional convoys were en route, I released the entire crew shortly after lunch, which was about five hours early. I remained behind just in case a few vehicles straggled in. This practice was quite different from most managers who lead other shops because it seemed as though most took pleasure in never offering any relief for their people.

The next day was more of the same complaints—this time, from the team's only female member, a forty-nine-year-old retired US Army Sergeant First Class. Her complaints were no more legitimate than those previously made by forty-five-year-old also retired US Army Axel. I think the two of them played off each other, setting the tone for an uneasy work environment. Both of these workers understood that overseas contracting companies were not in a hurry to create employment vacancies because it was very hard to fill these vacancies. They were also aware that it would take much more than being a disruptive or disgruntled employee to be fired. That being said, often my job was similar to that of a babysitter. I did not allow the fretful actions of these subordinates to impede on the team as a whole; thus, once again, the team was released early when the work was done.

It appeared that the team members always took advantage and were happy whenever I presented the opportunity to leave work early. What I did not know, however, was that some of these same members would report my practice of *early release* to my superiors, and any other smut they could manufacture concerning my leadership. To this day, I am not sure why there was such resistance from my team members. Perhaps the *crabs-in-a-barrel syndrome* fit the bill. If you are not familiar with that saying, it means a person who doesn't want anyone else to advance higher than him—or herself will pull the advancing person down as soon as that person begins to press forward. Nonetheless, I was never approached by upper management concerning my *early-release* practice; therefore, it continued.

One day, I got the word from my superiors that my unit would be sent a significantly larger number of convoy trucks that needed the jammer equipment removed in a short period of time. To aid in expediting this increase, five additional members were added to my team. All the new members were in their late twenties and were good workers with a positive nature. Early on, they expressed enjoyment in working in an atmosphere that allowed workers to leave early when the work was done. As you would have it in any work environment, word got out to some of the new members about the moaning going on from forty-five-year-old Axel about the facilitation of the work center and short workdays. One of the young men approached Axel and commented to him, "If a man gave me that much time off almost every day, I would have nothing negative to say about him, brother, you need to grow up."

A few days later, Axel was temporarily moved to another facility that was undermanned. Once away, it became apparent to me that Axel realized just how good he had it under my leadership. Axel was now working twelve full hours every day. So now the humbled Axel called me every few days, inquiring if I could do anything that would allow him to return to the work center. Eventually, Axel was allowed to return. He was a new man with a new attitude and motivation to conduct himself—time off.

Looking back on that time, I am sure there are some things that I could have done differently. Nonetheless, I must also admit that there are some people you just cannot help. In this case, help came in the form of time off, yet the forty-year-old needed the twenty-year-old to say it before it could be realized. It is hard to fathom how anyone would complain about working half days while continuing to receive the same pay.

Chapter Eight
CHURCH MEMBERS

Brenda was one of my more religious cousins and who was an active member of one of the churches in her city. Though her personal and business schedule was quite demanding, she would submit to the call for help whenever she could. One of her fellow church members, Sister Martha, had previously volunteered to singlehandedly run the church youth program. A week into the program, Sister Martha realized how challenging the assignment was and thus appealed to the congregation for assistance in running the program.

The call for help from Sister Martha was echoed in the church business meeting and Sunday-morning announcements by a church official or chancellor, but still there was no rush of volunteers. Brenda heard the call for help and could not bear seeing Sister Martha so overwhelmed. Therefore, she volunteered to help but made it clear to the church leaders and Sister Martha that she could only do so in an interim capacity and for only 120 days due to the assignments associated with her pursuit of a doctorate degree.

Brenda was satisfied with the system she and Sister Martha had established, and things were progressing nicely. As the third month drew to an end, Brenda reminded the church that time was soon approaching when she would no longer be able to assist with the program. Brenda might as well have been speaking to a wall because none of the church leaders, including Sister Martha, made any moves toward finding a replacement for her. Instead, the only thing they did was plead with my cousin repeatedly to extend her time with the program. Finally, my cousin surrendered and informed them that she would extend for three more weeks, but that would be all. The program was now interfering with her predetermined plans.

The three weeks went by, and the church still had no successor for Brenda. Therefore, at this point, she had no choice but to leave the position. They again tried to change her mind, but this time, to no avail; you see, the church duties had already started interfering with her doctorate program requirements.

Over a six-month period, the doctorate program and various other events occurring in Brenda's life at that time caused her to drastically reduce her time spent at the church. During her absence, there was no shortage of negative comments from the church community that eventually made it to her ears. Based on the nature of the comments, some of the church members seemed to have a genuine disdain toward her. The general attitude concerning Brenda's exit was that she had not only turned her back on them but also on God.

When Brenda returned to the church, the first person she saw was the preacher's wife, who greeted her with a very warm embrace. The preacher's wife commented to her at that moment, "God said he wants all of you. God said education is good, but he wants all of you."

Remember, just months earlier, the person delivering these strong words from God is the same person who referred to Brenda as not being on the right side of God. According to Brenda, it is no secret that between the preacher and his wife, the highest degree is an associate degree. I seriously doubt that God would divinely tell that woman that my cousin should be focusing on volunteering in their youth program instead of professionally preparing herself in her career. After all, as the old saying goes, "God helps those who help themselves." To date, Brenda has not returned to that church.

The only action Brenda was guilty of was hearing of a situation that needed attention and rendering help for it. She even took additional measures by extending her help past her original cutoff period. In spite of the fact that no one else from the church congregation stepped up to assist, they found the time to give life to a position that fostered such disdain that voiced she had turned her back on God. There are no limits to the enemies one can obtain by simply helping, and today, they can even be found in the church.

Chapter Nine
THE HIGH COST OF INDEPENDENCE

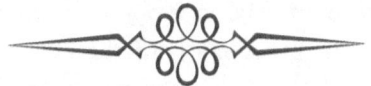

My wife's great-aunt Mama Fay is in good health for someone who is now in her early eighties, but good health can sometimes be a matter of perspective for a person of that age. I draw this conclusion because the garden work that she does in the heat of the day burns her light skin. She has major hearing loss but refuses to accept a hearing aid; she has cataracts in one eye but refuses to have it repaired, and she is very thin and is losing weight. My wife had scheduled many doctor appointments with the focus to address these medical issues for her, but she always found an excuse not to go. I think we all give her a pass, given her age. We all understand her fears; we only urge but never force the needed surgery and apparatus assistance.

Her husband had passed away about ten years ago, and their only child's untimely death occurred about fifteen years before his father's. Over the years, my wife and some of her siblings shared the responsibilities of their aunt's needs, but once she reached her seventies, more attention to her well-being was required.

One of my wife's brothers lives in the same city as their aunt; the others are scattered across the country. On a visit one summer, my wife and I noticed that her aunt's house was at a point of serious distress, in need of major repair and reconstruction. Therefore, my wife scheduled a meeting via conference with all her siblings on the matter of their aunt's dwelling. A second face-to-face meeting took place at Mama Fay's house at Thanksgiving, which was the next time everyone was in town. Mama Fay was in attendance. During the meeting, all the problems with the house were identified. Mama Fay was delighted that the help would be coming. At the same time, during the meeting, Mama Fay made it clear that she needed to direct the project. We all concurred that this was not a good idea; it was pretty much a deal breaker. We all love her dearly, but we all know how difficult and fastidious she could be. In the past, whenever any of us tried to oversee or conduct smaller, everyday maintenance projects, she interfered so much that the projects stalled and were sometimes never completed. The projects that were able to be completed took twice as long as the normal time to finish. Thus, for a project of this magnitude to be successful, we could not allow her to be involved in the direction process.

An additional problem to this project existed. Mama Fay had developed into a hoarder. Over the years, these behaviors have led to deterioration of some areas of the dwelling structure and insect and rodent infestation. Clearly, the first order of business was to declutter and clean. Again, we all knew she would fight us no matter what action we took to resolve these problems that she did not know existed, but out of love, we had to do what was necessary to bring her living conditions to a safe and sanitized level.

After several other strategizing meetings, a plan was born. Due to work schedules, all of us would only be available to come together the week before Christmas holiday. You see, every year at Christmas, Mama Fay would always spend that week with one of her nephews. Therefore, once she was picked up for this annual event, we would spring *Operation Saving Mama Fay* into action. In order for this project to be completed in the short span of time we were allotted, in addition to all the siblings, we called upon every family member available to lend a helping hand toward the facilitation of this project; extra workers were also hired.

Once everyone was in place, we pounced on sorting and removing debris. To lend some insight as to the magnitude of debris, after seven hours, we had filled one commercial-size Dumpster from one room alone. A subsequent second and third Dumpster would have to be ordered to complete the task. Once enough debris had been removed, we could finally evaluate the full extent of repairs needed. Upon evaluation, it was discovered that two walls located at the back end of the house had to be removed and replaced because they had rotted away. New floors were ordered, painters hired, windows repaired and draped with new fashions, and several plumbing issues were addressed. The project evolved into a beautiful display of unadulterated love and genuine concern for Mama Fay. Help poured in from many avenues, as well as the project fathered a deeper bond between all family members who assisted.

Finally, the day came for Mama Fay to return home from her holiday visit with her nephew. On the ride home, Mama Fay was informed that a face-lift had been done to her home. Patiently awaiting her arrival for the big reveal were two of my wife's brothers and their wives. Having already returned home to our home several states away, my wife and I monitored the situation over the phone as it unfolded.

Finally, she walked in, and everyone yelled, "Surprise!" And what a surprise it was. From the onset, she appeared very happily surprised. Mama Fay was bursting with positive comments about how nice of a face-lift her home had received. She went from room to room, inspecting and commenting on how well she loved everything. To top things off, both of the brothers' wives had prepared a huge meal for all in attendance.

As I stated earlier, we all knew this project would be a hard sell to Mama Fay, and we were really concerned about how she would react to our efforts. We were all relieved to see Mama Fay's reaction and hear her comments. What a joyous time! What a happy day! What a celebration! What a blissful gathering! That is, until it dawned on her that the new, clean, decluttered, and remodeled space came at the cost of removing years of items she had collected. Even though 90 percent of the items removed were garbage and rodent-infested items, to her they were *her* garbage and rodent-infested items.

It was the next morning when my wife called to check on Mama Fay that lowered the boom on all of us. She was fighting mad. "None of you had any right to get rid of my stuff," she complained. My wife and I tried fruitlessly to explain to Mama Fay that we saved all items worth saving, boxed and labeled them, and discarded everything that was pure trash or rodent infested. Mama Fay responded, "I have no more of an animal problem in my house than any of you have in yours." Sadly, this just was not true. The rodent problem was bad enough to possibly pose a health problem. We were planning to do other aesthetic things to the house, but since my Mama Fay was so outraged by what we had already done, we would not dare attempt to change anything else until she calmed down.

The scolding lasted for a few weeks, and none of the participants were spared her rage. Finally, after being immersed in another scolding call with her aunt, my wife tried a different approach: she asked Mama Fay if she could find it in her heart to forgive us all for what we had done. Mama Fay is a woman with strong Christian faith; that statement spoke to her heart, and at that moment, she vowed to forgive her family for invading her space without her permission.

Mama Fay was struggling as hard as she could to hang on to as much independence as possible, but the clash occurred when her health and well-being did not agree with her wishes. There was no one else to do what had to be done; therefore, we had to take over. The house was in grave disrepair, unsanitary, and with animals and insects she could not hear or see. We all understood that our help would potentially set the stage whereby Mama Fay would have to deal with varied emotions like denial, embarrassment, anger, and hurt. But everything comes with a price, and in this case, this just was the high cost of Mama Fay maintaining her independence.

Chapter Ten
THAT OLD CAR

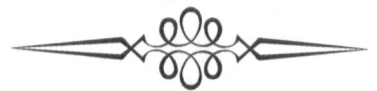

My friend Dale went through a very painful and economically draining divorce after a marriage of twenty years. Though he and his wife had been having issues, he really was not prepared for the separation. And to make matters worse, shortly after the divorce was final, he lost his job. Things only got worse for Dale. Soon after the loss of his job, his late-model car became the next casualty—it was repossessed. Since transportation was a must and his finances were limited, Dale purchased the only thing he could afford, a large very old car. Dale has always been a very proud man, so much so that I think it may have been to his detriment. That's why it never surprised me when my offers to help were never accepted. But as his friend, he did rely on me for sanity checks—that is, he needed to vent a lot; therefore, we talked several times a day during this time.

One spring day, I received an unannounced visit from Dale. He looked troubled and in poor health. We shared a meal and somber conversation that day, and at the end of the meal, Dale asked me for a loan. I had no reservations about granting the request. I just wanted to help in any way I could. Still, Dale felt obligated to tell me he would return the money in two days. Sadly, I did not hear from Dale in two days; in fact, it would be months before I would hear from him again.

A few months later, a chance meeting happened. I met Dale's mother in the grocery store. After salutations between us, I asked her how her son was doing. She informed me Dale was in Dallas, working on a job. We engaged in a few minutes of casual conversation, then Dale's mother offered me his son's new telephone number. I accepted, and we parted ways.

When I contacted Dale later that evening, he was glad to hear from me. He mentioned he was sorry about not paying the money back but was too embarrassed to contact me until he had the money and was back on his feet. He voiced he initially found a job when he first moved there, but after about a month, he was laid off. I told him not to worry about returning any funds until he had his finances squared away. Then with a nervous tremble in his voice, Dale uttered, "Man, after several months of being single and unemployed with limited funds, I found himself living out of my car. And you know me, being as stubborn as I am, it took me months to solicit help from anyone." This news was earth-shattering to me. He also expressed that he was careful not to let his two teenage sons see him in that situation because it was not the best example of being a man. Dale went on to explain that he had initially gone to Dallas for shelter because he was living out of his car. Shelter was provided by his aunt Kathy. Also residing in the house was Walter, Aunt Kathy's thirty-one-year-old son.

Our conversation went on for hours; Dale seemed to have so much to unveil. I agonized for my friend as I listened attentively to this forty-seven-year-old man who was desperately trying to piece his life back together. He described his aunt's neighborhood as quite a bit more hostile than where he once lived with his family, and the environment inside the home was not much better. In spite of paying the rent he could afford to his aunt for living there, much of the food he purchased and placed in the refrigerator was often eaten by Walter.

Dale described Walter as a character. Dale divulged to me that Walter was on his third car in a five-month period, having totaled each of them in an accident or just being plain callous. One morning when Walter's car would not start, he asked Dale to taxi him to his job, in which he did. Soon after, Walter's continued reckless handling of his car eventually caused it to stop functioning. So of course, the next time he had to go to work, he asked Dale; but this time, when he asked, Dale simply gave him the keys. Surprisingly, at the end of the day, Walter returned home with the car intact. But when Dale asked for his key back, Walter informed Dale he was planning on going over to his girlfriend's house. Dale told him that the use of his car was a one-time deal to be used only to go to work, not clear across town to socialize. Walter seemed to justify his actions by relaying to Dale that he put gas in the car and all the gas had not been used. Dale responded to Walter by telling him, "Thanks for the gas, but you should be thanking me for the loan of the car."

Dale's story was compelling; he went on to say that when Walter's mother returned home, Walter complained to his mother how Dale was being unfair with his car. Once Aunt Kathy had sorted out the events in her mind, she told Dale that if another event such as that one occurred, he would have to leave because she couldn't have him upsetting her son. "Not only that," Dale angrily voiced, "last week, Aunt Kathy asked me to cosign on a loan for Walter to get a car, and I told her an emphatic *no*." I interrupted Dale with this remark, "Before you loaned your cousin your car, you were at least treading water in the pool of life, but you started to drown once you attempted to help him with your car. What is it about that old wheeled piece of metal? It first served as a shelter for you, and now it is an object directly related to the removal of you from your shelter." I would tread lightly when it came to helping Walter. Helping a selfish, ungrateful person such as he to swim only requires one remedy: he needs to swim alone.

Chapter Eleven
A CHILLY GAME CHANGER

Ever since *Operation Saving Mama Fay* occurred, the family determined to replace Mama Fay's refrigerator, which was in poor condition and barely keeping her food at a safe temperature. Therefore, we planned to replace the fridge the next time we would be in town visiting, which happened to be Mothers' Day. My wife felt Mother's Day would be a great time to give a gift.

We arrived in town two days before Mother's Day, plenty of time to shop for and arrange delivery of the refrigerator. Therefore, my wife and I purchased the fridge, but due to time constraints, we had to include my brother in the process. My brother picked up the refrigerator from the home improvement store, and later that evening, I would borrow his truck and install it in Mama Fay's house.

In the meantime, Mama Fay, my wife and I, my wife's sister and her son were enjoying dinner out at the invitation of one of Mama Fay's cousins. Reflecting on Mama Fay's reaction to our last efforts to help, my wife and I agreed that surely this effort would be different; after all, it was a gift and not an invasion of property. My nephew was aware of the condition of his much-older relative's refrigerator and was glad to know we had purchased her a new one. He also expressed to me during dinner how glad he thought his great-great-aunt would be to receive a new refrigerator because she really needs it. I then responded to him, "Sometimes, you make your biggest enemies when you help someone." My nephew shook his head in disbelief then chuckled, "Uncle, that doesn't make sense, I don't believe that. Why would anyone get mad at you when you try to help them?" I responded to him in a lighthearted manner, "You will see one day, nephew, one day you will see."

We all had a pleasant dinner. On the way home from dinner, our plan was to drop by my brother's house, pick up the fridge, and then install it at Mama Fay's. My wife's idea was to break the surprise to Mama Fay in the car on the way from the restaurant. Everything worked out according to plan. Mama Fay seemed well pleased with her dinner that day, and the biggest gift was on the brink of being presented. Therefore, once we arrived at Mama Fay's house, my wife gave me the thumbs-up on the gift.

However, just as quick as I got the thumbs-up on the fridge, Mama Fay had done a complete 180-degree turn. Before the senior exited the vehicle, she started in on my wife, fussing and complaining about us changing her plans for the evening with the addition of the refrigerator installation. "I like things done when I want them done, and I told you I don't like surprises. If you and your husband wanted to give me a refrigerator, you could have just given me the money, and I would have bought it on my own time," she continued. In the midst of Mama Fay's ranting and raving, my nephew uttered to me, "I did not think my great-great-aunt could speak with such anger. Now I see what you meant, uncle, when you said, *if you want to make an enemy, try and help someone.*" After witnessing my great-aunt's latest meltdown of fighting against those who were trying to help her, I told my sister-in-law to tell her that if it would make her happy, we would leave immediately and take the fridge back to the store. But my aunt responded in a slightly calmer manner, "That doesn't make any sense since you already brought it."

With that being said, we proceeded on with the removal of the old and installation of the new refrigerator. After a continual tongue-lashing, we finally finished the transition of transferring her food and was ready to plug in the fridge, only to discover that the power cord was on the opposite side than that of the fridge we just removed; thus, the plug could not reach the nearest electrical outlet. Upon this discovery, the senior voiced, "You two really don't know what you are doing because you got me a refrigerator with a cord that is too short." Now there was nothing wrong with the length of the refrigerator cord; instead, there was something wrong with the location of the electrical outlets about five feet from the floor in this old house. Thank goodness for industrial extension cords.

In our eyes, we had a serious quality-of-life mission to perform and a short time to accomplish it. We weighed the pros and the cons of executing this mission, and in the big scheme of things, the tongue-lashings were painful, but it was far less painful than her continued use of that poorly performing appliance. Mama Fay's anger aside, the actions we took out of love could have very easily saved her life; the refrigerator was a chilly game changer.

Chapter Twelve

MORE AGONIZING THAN ANY ENEMY

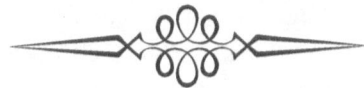

After being in the military for a little more than four years, I received an assignment of choice in Alabama. About a month into my new assignment, one day my supervisor released me two hours early for the day because the work was slow. Traffic was unusually high that day for it to be two o'clock in the afternoon on a Tuesday. I was traveling south and positioned on the inside lane of a four-lane highway when the light turned red. Fast approaching me was an older lady with her left-turn blinker on. She was attempting to turn, but since traffic was so heavy, she would be there for a while if I would not assist her to turn.

Therefore, I prematurely stopped and left a gap open between the car in front of me and my car and waved her on so that she could proceed. The old woman looked at me and rendered a gracious smile, and I, in turn, smiled back. Then she aggressively accelerated into the open space with a left turn. As her car accelerated in front of me, instinctively, I looked in my rearview mirror to appraise the positioning of traffic behind me. I was hoping she would stop in front of me and look before venturing on. I was powerless to do anything at this point to stop what was potentially about to occur.

Well, everything was put in motion, and she drove right through the space that I provided in front of my car without checking the other lane, and *pow*! She got T-boned on her passenger side. No one was seriously hurt, and she exited her car. In my attempt to simply render some driver courtesy to a fellow driver on the city streets, an accident occurred. The woman gave me a long stare as if I tried to make the accident happen. In essence, she did not proceed properly; in fact, she proceeded haphazardly. I'm not sure whether or not I made an enemy that day, but if I did, I was only attempting to help. The blame I felt that day because of the aid I was attempting to render went very wrong and was far more agonizing for me than any enemy I might have made.

Chapter Thirteen

I DROPPED MY CELL PHONE

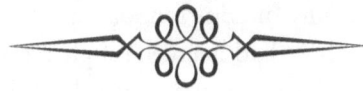

Of all the chapters assembled in this book thus far, this chapter's story is the one example of helping that really stings in a completely different way and, as a result, inspired this book. This passage took place in March of 2013 when I was presented with an offer to explore a time-share presentation with a company while on vacation in Las Vegas. I had already planned a weekend of events for my wife's upcoming birthday, so I figured the events of the presentation could only add spice to an already event-filled day trip.

We planned the trip in a way that would give us plenty of time to explore the area prior to our appointment. After enjoying our time exploring the area, we still managed to arrive at our appointment thirty minutes early. One hour later, we were still waiting to be assigned to an agent in spite of several couples arriving much later than us and already being assigned one. Finally, I mentioned to my wife, "Have you noticed that we are the only members of our ethnic group here?" "No, I did not pay much attention to that," she responded. I continued, "I am willing to bet that the reason it is taking so long to assign us to an agent is probably because they are trying to match us up with an agent who matches our ethnic group. Being that I have only seen one such agent, I'll bet we won't get assigned until he finishes with his customer." About twenty more minutes elapsed, and other couples were starting their presentations; many had arrived after us. Normally, when faced with such bias-type situations, I would either leave or make a complaint and then leave. But out of curiosity, I wanted to see how this one was going to play out. In addition, based on how this scenario was unfolding, if there had been the slightest real possibility of me buying a time-share that day, it was long gone.

Finally, a man with a warm grin and a pleasant demeanor walked up to us and said, "Hi, I'm Sonny McRoberts, and I will be providing you a tour of our facility today." And yes, Sonny was a member of the same ethnic group as the two of us. Sonny escorted us to the gathering room where the three of us and many other agents and couples sat and got acquainted. During that time was when I revealed that that day was my wife's birthday. Sonny then revealed that his birthday had just past a few days earlier. Then I joined in and revealed that my birthday was four days away; it seemed as though this all March birthday gathering was pure destiny. As the cross flow of information continued, Sonny revealed that he was retired from the Army and had spent time in the Middle East as a contractor. My wife glanced over at me with a small grin because she knew what I was about to reveal. At which point, I shared with Sonny that I was also a retired military member, but I was in the Air Force and had also been a contractor in the Middle East. We shared so much I'm sure my wife secretly hoped we would stop sharing and soon return to the nature of our visit there, the presentation. After discovering how much in common I had with Sonny, it seemed as if I had known him for years. Though we all agreed we could spend the day conversing, Sonny was at work, and his job was to sell us a time-share.

Sonny was very efficient at his craft; he gave us a solid presentation. I thanked Sonny for his efforts and then informed him that in spite of his proficiency, we were sure that we would not be buying his product today. I also informed him that he should filter us through the process as quickly as he could so that we would not hinder him from a potential buyer. I felt awful about taking up so much of Sonny's time, but once we had been presented with all the information, my wife and I knew we were not interested in purchasing the product. With that being said, I whispered to Sonny, "All is not lost today because I can provide you with some valuable information about real-estate investing that will make a difference in your life at zero cost to you." "Sounds interesting and I am open to hear more," Sonny responded. Sonny helped us sail through the rest of the process, and then we exchanged numbers, and I agreed to contact him later.

I wanted to make good on my promise to Sonny. Consequently, a few weeks later, while visiting relatives in California, I contacted Sonny and informed him that if he could meet me at a location between the two areas, I would start my real-estate teaching session with him. Without hesitation, Sonny accepted my offer, and we agreed to meet at a centrally located restaurant.

Sonny was enthusiastic about our meeting—that's why I was a little puzzled as to why he attended our training session without so much as a pad and pencil. Nevertheless, I managed to retrieve a pen and an old piece of paper from my car, and we moved on. Unlike our first introduction of sharing life experiences, this session was packed full with business information and lasted about two hours.

Over the next few weeks, Sonny contacted me often via cell phone with many questions, and I provided many answers. About six weeks after our first meeting, I set up a second face-to-face meeting with Sonny to continue the real-estate training.

This meeting was much more intense. I passed out pamphlets, and this time, Sonny had a pen, paper, and tape recorder. I brought in two identical manuals of past real-estate boot camps that I had attended in the past. I expressed to Sonny that my original plan was to give him one of the manuals, but second thought dictated I transfer all essential information between manuals first so that neither one of us would be deprived of any pertinent information. As well, I knew I would be returning to the area soon and would be able to pass off the manual at that time. During the meeting, I was pleasantly surprised to learn that Sonny had already found a potential real-estate deal and wanted my feedback; I provided it, of course. His diligence was a great testament to me because his action proved I had already made an impact on someone who, before our meeting, had no prior knowledge and is now utilizing that knowledge.

Before we concluded this three hour training session, to show his gratitude, Sonny gave me $5,000 worth of Iraqi dinars (about $5 US dollars). I attempted to give it back to him, but he would not accept it back. He suggested, "Please let me finally bless you since you are constantly blessing me." Since he put it that way, I agreed to accept it and assured him I would place it in my Bible. I repeated an earlier comment to Sonny, "I am just trying to help someone in need of help. I will never charge you a dime. I will get my blessings later for helping you,

I always do. I'm just doing my part of what we are all supposed to do—apply the golden rule by helping someone as I would like to be helped."

Nine days later, Sonny contacted me about the real-estate deal he first introduced to me at our last meeting. Only now, he needed instruction on how to put the deal together. I immediately jumped in by sending Sonny some examples of purchase and sales contracts via e-mail links. Then I explained to him that we would discuss how to fill out the forms later that evening. As we discussed the property, Sonny informed me on what he projected to net on the offer. Analyzing Sonny's description of the property clearly showed to me that he was not asking enough for the property. To aid in my assessment, I asked him to send me some pictures of the property. In addition, I informed Sonny that I may be interested in the property if, for some strange reason, his investors fall through.

Later that evening, we continued our discussion about the property. I had already received the photos I requested of Sonny, but they were only internal photos and no photos of the exterior of the property. Thus, I asked Sonny to provide me with the address of the property so that I could see the neighborhood from Google Earth. At that moment, the phone went silent for about fifteen seconds and then hung up. I immediately called back, but the phone went straight to voice mail. I repeatedly attempted to reconnect with Sonny for about fifteen minutes but again had no results. Stunned by the peculiar disconnection, I related to my wife, "I am 99 percent sure that this guy thinks I am trying to steal his deal." She remained optimistic about the situation, but I persisted that there were too many coincidental events that led me to this conclusion.

About two and a half hours later, Sonny sent me a text message. This is the actual message from Sonny McRoberts:

"Dropped my phone on hard surface. Malfunctioning now. Not charging still need form Talk later." My contention was not that the story may not have been true, but if the phone had truly malfunctioned, he had options. He could have communicated with me via his wife's phone. And if he was unable to use a different phone that night, surely there were phones at his place of employment or perhaps a coworker who would have been willing to let him use his or her phone.

Finally, four days later, on Father's Day, I received a text from Sonny stating, "Happy Father's Day." If there was any doubt of my previous position, this text proved I was right. Before the "I dropped my cell phone" incident, Sonny always communicated with me verbally, but since that time, there has only been text. The next day, I communicated back with a text that stated, "Thanks for the Father's Day salutation."

The following day, Sonny sent another text stating, "Check your e-mail Sir." Out of curiosity, I checked my e-mail, and wouldn't you know it, seven days later, there were pictures of the property, an address, and other information I had not even inquired about. Sonny revealed everything. His property was under contract, and therefore (in his head), I was no longer a threat of stealing his deal. At this point, this action proved nothing more than he clearly did not trust me. I believe Sonny suffered quite a loss that day because the trust issues that he possessed had caused him to trade away future mentoring and other investment technique lessons in the future for one little deal. So whatever monetary amount he expected from the deal, God bless him, and I hope he gets it, because if he did not, he traded away everything and received nothing.

I haven't heard from Sonny since his last text to me. But that last text spoke volumes. The verbiage he used appeared that he had not classified me as an enemy after helping him, but rather, it looked as if he was attempting to reestablish a contact link he had destroyed. But now, it is far too late for any reconciliation because I now clearly see the type of individual he is. So in this case, I don't think I made an enemy after helping someone—instead, the insult of mistrust and offensive actions displayed by him placed him uniquely on my enemy list.

Chapter Fourteen

DISTINGUISHING BETWEEN A HELPER AND AN ENEMY

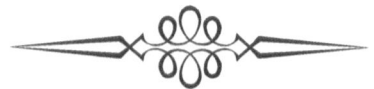

The passages prior to this point have been experiences I have either personally experienced, or experiences of family, friends and associates; but this final chapter has a broader tone. If one were to take a wide angled view of our nation's current course of events to the subject of *helping those who later classify you as an enemy,* related issues would be worthy of a chapter in this book. As the following paragraphs unfold I will address the notion of help at a national level.

There are millions of Americans in the United States today void of basic health care coverage. Perhaps the fundamental reason for this lack of coverage is simply the skyrocketing cost of healthcare in this country. Over the years the various issues related to healthcare cost and coverage has become a subject of great political debate, confusion and suffrage in the United States; and the ugly truth is while the debate goes on; many citizens will lose their lives from many preventative health conditions that could have been averted by a single preventive health care examination. It does not matter what biases you bring to the table, if you are one of the millions at present without healthcare when this assistance arrives it should be considered. However, if one cannot recognize assistance when it indeed arrives, there is little anyone can do to assist.

The United States have the capability to drop bombs on any target anywhere in the world deemed necessary. But just as we have the powers to destroy any target we also have the capability to aid at will to any nation on that same global stage. Therefore, it is safe to say that our nation's report card on rendering assistance is clear, we can and do help anyone at anytime and anywhere we choose. Yet, with all the capabilities to render help at our fingertips, we perhaps do the poorest job helping domestically when it comes to the subject of health care. We have made good strides in the past and have successfully enacted some specific measures to address unique areas of healthcare. But as great of a nation as we are to date we cannot seem to agree on a national healthcare solution.

I am sure that most Americans can recite an example of someone who has been negatively affected by our health care system. Once when one of my friends had a medical emergency he was rushed to the nearest hospital emergency room. My friend had no healthcare coverage but since medical facilities are required to render aid to all who arrive, he received it. A few hours later a stent had been placed in his heart and he was resting quietly in a hospital room.

A life was saved that day but since he had no health insurance, who incurred the cost of this uninsured US citizen? Does the hospital simply absorb the cost? Does the doctor or nurse simply not get paid for the life saving service that was provided? The answer is the American taxpayer pays! If you pay taxes your tax dollar pays for those who cannot afford their own health care. Since we are paying for the uninsured anyway, does it not stand to reason that with a plan that cost would be lowered? Canada has health care plans for all of its citizens. And as I stated earlier, as a nation we can do much better; than the uninsured citizens with no other choice than to arrive at the emergency rooms of America with no health care plan.

The Patient Protection and Affordable Care Act (PPACA) commonly called the Affordable Care Act (ACA) or Obama Care is governments answer to a universal plan of health care. It was passed into by congress and signed by President Obama on March 23, 2010. The plan was birthed to address the millions of Americans who desire health care coverage but have been denied.

However, after the law was passed, the opposition of the new health care law challenged its constitutionality. After the challenge of its legality, the PPACA was upheld by the supreme court. However, opponents of the new law still waged opposition against the tool that offered potential solutions for health care previsions to millions of Americans.

During the 2008 presidential election Senator Obama promised healthcare reform and was elected president. This matter became the political focal point of the next presidential race in 2012. Casting a vote for the President would support the continuation of his signature achievement, the Patient Protection and Affordable Care Act. As well, a vote for the presidential hopeful would allow him to fulfill his promise to repeal the Health Care Law;

As the bid for the White House continued in the 2012 campaigns, the president would voice on many occasions that everyone should be allowed to have affordable health care; as for the president's opponent he would never get his chance to repeal the new health care law after the president was reelected. Since the President's goal was to help, my own experience had shown me that it was only a matter of time before the people that he was attempting to help would label him as their health care foe.

Not to my surprise, as the opposition to the health care plan increased, anger, confusion, ignorance and unfounded accusations ensued. In some instances corporations expressed forced impending layoff a year in advance of the initiation of the health care plan.

Predicting layoffs a year in advance under these circumstances was somewhat questionable, but not to be outdone, in 2012 a new Hampshire state representative expressed disdain for the law by making one of the most bizarre statements; his words were *"What is Obama Care? It is a law that is just as destructive as to personal and individual liberty as a Fugitive Slave Act of 1850 that allowed slave owner to come to New Hampshire to seize African Americans in the federal courts."*

Now you would think that the biggest opponent of the health care reform would be the presidential candidate and his supporters who vowed to repeal it. But after a long campaign of the health care laws opposition defining of the new health care law, it appeared the biggest opponents of the Affordable Health Care Act were the people who needed it the most. How dare the president force health care down my throat one person complained. I could only pause and then smile; here we go again I thought. The president is attempting to help and in his quest, he has developed some enemies.

Stop and ask you self this question; Why would anyone who presently have no health care resist a vehicle that would make it affordable for them? Answer; confusion. Opposition commercials and billboard ads have muddied up the waters so bad that when help arrived it was not recognizable for those who needed it. If one cannot recognize the help when it indeed arrives, there is little anyone can do to help.

There is an old saying that goes alone the lines of *"Ignorance being Bliss."* But being uninformed on health care matters can do harm. This type of ignorance is definitely not bliss, it actually can be the cause of your demise.

Regardless of what ethnic group or political party affiliation that you align yourself with, if you are a person who cannot afford health care it would seem logical (at least to me) for you to be a proponent for health care reform. If you have a pre existing condition that causes you to be uninsurable, from where I sit you should be one of the programs biggest fans. Preventive health care measure will save millions of lives, but if you cannot decipher the helper and the enemy, the painful life lesson of taking the wrong action will in most cases cause further problems. With the number of people who will surely die without many of the preventative health care treatments, the time for this help is now

In September 2013, an Illinois senator voices a completely different outlook of healthcare reform than the earlier referenced senator of 2012. The senator from Illinois expressed *"We are going forward with the health care reform that's a good thing and it's good for America so that many people currently without health insurance will have it for the first time in their lives and the policies that all of us buy will be worth more, they won't be reject kids with preexisting conditions for example, that's a good thing."* If the Affordable Care Act was as bad as claimed, why not simply leave it alone and it will fail on its own as with any poor law, if that is truly what it is. But it would seem the opponents of this law are more fearful that it just may succeed.

When you make up your mind to help, you must be careful because with help comes responsibilities. I am not suggesting for anyone to enable any person by simply helping too much as noted in the introduction when referring to teaching a man to fish instead of continually giving him one. In one aspect teaching someone to fish also occurs with the health care reform law because in both examples the fish is not given; as with most things of value there is a cost.

On the first day of the enrolment period for healthcare under the Affordable Care Act, the site, was overwhelmed and could not handle the traffic load. Because of the electronic systems inability to handle the massive amount of traffic, the opposition voiced that it already was a failure; that claim is premature. So it would appear the opposition's message did not stop the public in their choice of the healthcare program. However, the party line press from the healthcare reform opponents did confuse a number of healthcare hopefuls to the point of healthcare being unrecognizable. Just days before the first day of enrolment a survey was rebroadcasted on various media circuits that had recently occurred. When the participants of the survey were asked "Which healthcare program is better, Obama Care or the Affordable Care Act," most embraced the Affordable Care Act, but dismissed Obamacare because (in their words) Obamacare has just too many problems.

Even if you are the president of the United States, you can gain enemies by simply attempting to help. But the sad truth is some people you simply cannot help because many have not paid attention to the details to know that the Affordable Care Act and Obama Care are one in the same.

History will attest if this new healthcare law is a good or bad thing, but what's already know is, if you don't like a law there are already established procedures as to how the law is to be addressed; that process requires congress to submit actions to repeal it.

The question is, which entity is the helper and which entity is the enemy; a president who is attempting to provide healthcare for the millions of the uninsured, or the body of congress who opposed that help to the extent of shutting down our government system?

If you can't, distinguishing between the helper and an enemy it's time to start paying attention.

However, now that we are generally post Covid 19, enough time has passed to present enough evidence to start getting a clear picture of who the enemy is. For starters, the Affordable Care Act has shown to be, in one word "affordable." That is, if you live in a state that allows federal funds to supplement the cost. For those of us who live in a state that allows federal funds to supplement the cost are part of the millions who benefit by having the Affordable Health Care.

Sounds a little crazy, you bet it does. What state would not allow federal funds. Who would block millions of people from receiving affordable health care? The governors that who. The governors have convinced many of their citizens that government assisted healthcare is not a positive thing. "Obamacare is bad, it cost too much, or we just don't need it in our state. Just ask someone from the state of Kentucky. Kentuckians will inform you that they don't need or want Obama Care in their state. But little do many of them know, their Connect Healthcare is Obamacare, the name has simply been changed. So, who is the real enemy?

The following is a list of governors who block the Affordable Care Act:

Wisconsin
Wyoming
Texas
Tennessee
South Carolina

Mississippi
Kansas
Georgia
Florida
Alabama

Is the enemy the Health Care Act that allows health Care to be affordable?

or

Is the enemy any governor who impedes federal funds from being available from his citizens?

Again, more than two million United States citizens do not have the option to choose health care because their state leader blocks the funds. I don't think is matters what side of the argument you are on, to remain in the best health, heath care is required, and if you are blocking people for receiving it, it would appear you are indeed the enemy; disguised as the helper.

Chapter Fifteen
THE ENEMY FROM BEYOND

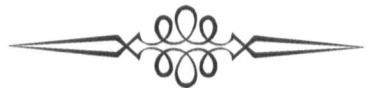

Taurus was a good-natured man who was as strong as the bull that symbolized his name. Many would describe his glorious wife Terri as a country girl because she was raised in the mountains. But being a mountain girl causes her to be well rounded with the ability to adapt to most situations. Together they were a glorious couple, and shortly after their first year of marriage they welcomed their first Son Tiberius.

Tiberius was wise and performed well in sports. Being sensible and like his father, he was well rounded and did not usually meet any strangers. The couple loved their first child and always did what they could for him. Tiberius in turn returned his devotion by doing all he could to help his parents. He was always grateful for the limited things his parents could do for him.

Oscar was two years younger than Tiberius. Unlike his older brother, Oscar entered the world with limited physical abilities, but the creator provided him with strong writing and verbal skills. Other than his mother Oscar was on occasion hard to have a good relationship with.

Bryan also performed well in sports and did well in academics. He had no trouble making friends, but that is the part of him that usually kept his parents guessing. Bryan possessed remarkable leadership skills but occasionally he associated with friends that did not care much about their learning. He was loyal to his parents and was thankful for what they did for him.

Laurence was the youngest of the four. By the time he was born his parents had many monetary systems in place. When he was in high school, his parents attempted to purchase him a used car, but he did not want it. Therefore, a new one was purchased. Generally, no matter what his parents purchased for him, he was not satisfied, but that did not keep his parents from trying to please him.

Time moved on and three of the four sons were now married with children of their own. After their mother became a great grandmother for the tenth time, she passed away. Tarus, their father, was alone for the first time in more than a half century. Bryan, now divorced and still living in town, moved in with his dad and ensured his father was well taken care of. Laurence also lived locally but did not visit much.

Tiberius and Oscar each lived in different states than their father. Tiberius came to town many times a year and coordinated with Bryan whenever he needed to leave town to ensure their elderly parent was cared for.

Years later after Taurus dies, his Will was read. Laurence seemed to glow with eagerness. Laurence knew that his father had put in his Will to leave Laurence all the cash within his bank account. His father left it all to him because he had told his father he did not want any other items.

Taurus had always done everything for his youngest son. The real estate was left to Tiberius and Bryan which was valued at half a million. The stock went to Oscar with a value of half a million. Finally, the monetary part of the Will finally was read. It was announced that all cash from the estate would be inherited solely by Laurence.

When Taurus fell ill, there was five million in his bank account. Taurus was ill for many years and his care reduced the amount in the account to just a few thousand. Laurence was now angry with his dad and calmly voiced his dad was not fair.

Taurus was aware that Laurence did not visit him much over the years and left him exactly what he had asked. By giving him what he had asked for, his father, in death had accidently set the stage to allow his youngest son to make him an enemy. The Enemy was from beyond.

Chapter Sixteen

WHEN A MAN DOES NOT WANT

Early one Saturday morning my cousin contacted me and asked if I could possibly fit her nephew into my new operation as a favor. He was twenty-eight years of age and lived with his mom. She also let me know he was having a hard time finding employment. She told me he was raised by a single parent, and he did not always have proper respect for authority. He had no car but since I was doing a favor for my cousin, I agreed to pick him up and teach him some carpentry skills.

On the first day of meeting the recruit, just after entering the car he uttered his name was Caleb. After a little, small talk he stated he was just a young man living life. Caleb slept all the way to the worksite. Moments after arriving at the site, I showed Caleb the first thing I did each day was open windows throughout the house for airflow. Then I showed him that the job entails installing drywall and if he learned this skill, he would have a much easier time finding work in the future.

My plan for Caleb the first day was for him to watch me cut and fit the drywall and as he assisted, he would learn. I would let him take the lead during the second half of the day. At lunchtime, Caleb had no food with him, so I took him to get some. He had no money, therefore I had to give him an advance. I informed Caleb that tomorrow he would need to bring lunch because we don't have the time to leave the site, order lunch, and drive him back at lunchtime. After lunch he was still not skilled enough to lead the task, therefore the training continued for the remainder of that workday. On the drive home I explain to him that from my perspective, it is up to us older men to teach or pull up the younger ones. But not much of that talk was received on the way home that day, because after one remark from him within the first five minutes, he was asleep.

On the second day he made no move to open the windows as I had previously shown him. I told him to cut a piece of drywall, but I discovered he did not understand how to read a ruler. My cousin had informed me that he was a high school dropout, but he should have gotten those basics much earlier. Being a person that does not like to give up on anyone who needs help and is trying, I explained to him how a ruler is read and somehow, he squirmed through it. Work did not go at the pace that it should have gone with two men, in fact, I would have moved at a faster pace by myself. At lunchtime he did not bring any food. At the end of the day I paid him again.

On the third day Caleb asked could I stop at a sandwich shop so he could get something to eat. I agreed. When we got to the restaurant, he asked could he borrow ten dollars. I had paid him at the end of the two previous days, nevertheless I gave him the advance. When he exited the restaurant, we had a twenty-minute drive ahead of us and he slept the entire way. When we arrived at the work site I exited the vehicle, unlocked the property, and began to open the windows. My thinking was, this was the third day, and he should know the routine by now. When I returned from opening the windows, I went to see why Caleb had not entered the house. Caleb was sitting on my tucks tailgate eating the sub sandwich.

I then voiced "Caleb this is how things are supposed to go. It is time to get to work, not to wait until we get to the site and start to eat." "But I'm hungry," he stated. "If you were hungry, the time to eat was in route to this location and not after we arrived. If you were serious about working, you would have exited the truck when I did. Why didn't you eat in route instead of after you got here?"

"I need you to take me home" Caleb voiced. "I sure will" I responded. I was glad to take him back to where I picked him up. Working with Caleb those three days was tough. He caused me to produce about half the outcome that I usually produce over a three-day period by myself.

I do not know of any job that will transport you round trip from residence to the job site, train you and pay you while you learn. If you find yourself with such an opportunity, the least you can do is be ready to work when the work is ready for you. If you are not ready to grab the opportunity when it presents itself, be assured, it will not hang around long or be handed to you.

It did not take long for Caleb to tell how unfair I was to him with a horrific version of why he quit working with me. Yes, I now have an enemy out there with Caleb for simply trying to help. However, I sleep very well each night, knowing that I did all I could to help. But if a man does not want anything you cannot make him want anything.

CONCLUSION

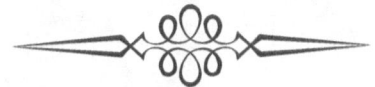

There are many passages in both the Old and New Testaments on matters of help.

"Do not withhold goods from those to whom it is due, when it is in your power to do it." Proverbs 3:27

"There will always be poor people in the land. Therefore I command you to be openhanded toward your brothers and toward the poor and needy in your land." Deuteronomy 15:11

So to all please understand, I am not recommending to anyone not to help; the scriptures clearly command us all to assist when we can and we are usually better when we do. I am merely suggesting that you think about the type of help you are going to render and consider the person you are attempting to help. Then determine how you are going to assist them and the implications of the assistance before you take the plunge. Sometimes help can cause an adverse effect, as with the old woman and the car accident. So consider your help wisely, because in the name of helping, you just may be causing a problem or, even worse, making an enemy. Understand that there are some people you simply cannot help; therefore, make sure you know how and when to help those that you can.

TEN POINTS OF ENEMIES AND HELP

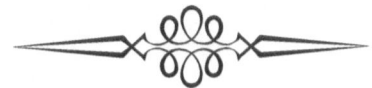

1. There are some people you just can't help.
2. In many instances, if you help, you will be blamed if all does not go well.
3. If someone receives something for free, often it has little value to them. Their actions will usually show that they will not appreciate it, but will destroy it, sell it cheap, give it away, or simply neglect it.
4. Often, people who ask for help don't need it.
5. The best things in life are free, but so are the worse things (enemies).
6. If a need is seen and help is ignored, it is just as bad as telling them you would not help.
7. Some who ask for help are not willing to help themselves.
8. Sometimes it is not clear if the extended hand is of an enemy or from someone to help.

9. Many times, people are their own worst enemy.
10. If you are your worst enemy, it does not matter if you are aware of it or not, because this type of person will always need to get prepared for an extremely bumpy ride. No matter how hard you run and attempt to hide, you will find that the person that you are attempting to elude will always be there. For anyone who meets this description or doesn't share my point of view, I challenge them to take the *glass test*.

Note: Before advising anyone to take such a crude test, I feel obligated to first give a strong word of caution to all.

INSTRUCTIONS FOR THE GLASS TEST

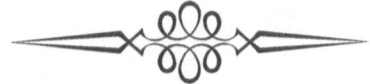

- To keep spillage to a minimum, it is recommended that the glass test be performed in the bathroom, with the door open.
- Next, ensure that the sink is filled with warm water and at least two clean towels are nearby to administer help if muscles become too tense.
- Ensure that there are no solids in the stool because sometimes the test can cause intense vomiting, and if this indeed occurs, this is not the time you will want to face solids.
- Ensure that the tub is filled with cold water just in case the situations presented are too powerful and they overcome you.
- Room lighting is an essential element as to the condition of your environment. This is most critical because it is essential that you have full view of the problem.

- Affix in your mind then ask yourself whether you help others or humbly accept it.
- Now step up to the big piece of glass that's usually positioned over the sink that has the power to reflect and is commonly called a mirror; look straight ahead.

The problem is staring directly at you. Now *fix it*!

www.ingramcontent.com/pod-product-compliance
Lightning Source LLC
LaVergne TN
LVHW092057060526
838201LV00047B/1432